The steps of a good man
are ordered by the Lord:
and he delighteth in his way.

Psalm 37:23

Along the Way

A collection of thoughts and inspirational verse

*To: Kay
With warm regards,
Carol Elaine*

Along the Way

A collection of thoughts and inspirational verse

Carol Elaine Powell

Sycamore Publishing Company

ALONG the WAY.
Copyright © 1999 by Carol Elaine Powell.

All rights reserved. No part of this book may be reproduced in any manner whatsoever without written permission except in the case of brief quotations embodied in critical articles or reviews.

Cover design by Alyson F. Flynn
Cover photography by Nancy J. Werner

Library of Congress Catalog Card Number: 98-90933
ISBN 0-9668750-2-8

Printed in the United States of America

10 9 8 7 6 5 4 3 2 1
   First Edition

For information address:
Sycamore Publishing Company
3450 St. Rd. 26 E.
P.O. Box 5842
Lafayette, IN 47903

E-mail: Sycamorepubl@earthlink.net
Website: home.earthlink.net/~Sycamorepubl

To my children…Joshua and Ryan,
who have taught me my life's true purpose,
and Claire, whose brief, gentle presence
forever touched my heart.

Contents

Preface XIII
Acknowledgments XV
Introduction XVII

    Come Walk with Me 1
    Follow Me 2
    Genesis 28:15 3
    Ecclesiastes 3:1-8 5

Chapter 1
PURPOSE 7

    Dare to Be 9
    Daybreak 10
    Awake! 11
    Morning 12
    The Artist 13
    Sunset 14
    That Eastern Light 15
    Extremes 16
    Landmark 18
    The Mighty Oak 19
    Thoreau quote 21

Chapter 2
LIFE 23

    Sharing 25
    A Miracle 26
    Child 28
    Claire 29
    One Solitary Rose 30
    The Opened Gift 31
    Love Lost 32
    Silver-hair Lady 34
    Mother's Love 35
    Gray Morning 36
    The Visit 37
    Shelley quote 39

Chapter 3
SEASONS 41

    Cycles 43
    The Place 44
    Solitude 45
    The Man 46
    A Witness 48
    Picking Corn 49
    Bringing in the Crops 50
    Harvest 52
    The Job 53
    The Season 54

Chapter 4
PROMISE 55

    words 57
    Blessings 59
    Moment of Truth 60
    The Unveiling 61
    Life's River 62
    words 63
    Angels 65
    Gentle Souls 66
    New Year's Eve 68
    A New Day 70

Chapter 5
MEMORIES 73

    words 75
    First Day 77
    Sleepless 78
    May Day Violets 79
    August Baseball 80
    Trail Ride 81
    Tranquillity 82
    The Clearing 83
    In the Barn 86
    Village Blacksmith 87
    The Town Jeweler 88
    The Carpenters 90

words 91
Dream Lights 93
Christmas 94
Christmas Morn 95
Fir 96
déjà vu 97
words 99

Chapter 6
QUESTIONS 101

Backwards 103
Restless Hearts 104
Questions 105
words 107
Fools 109
A Lonely Man 110
What If? 111
Stardust 112
words 113
Heaven's Sunset 115
The Flight 116
Airplane's View 117
words 119
My Secret 121
A Place 122
Escape 123
Thoreau quote 125

Chapter 7
LOVE 127

Sounds of Love 129
Gold 130
Lover's Moon 131
A Gift 132
Love 133
A Kiss 134
The Missing Part 136
"Hope" 137
Love Thoughts 138
Divided Heart 139
Questioned Love 140

The Runner's Soul 142
Safe 144
A Race 146
One Moment 147
Impasse 148
Silver Vase 150
Infidelity 151
Timing 152
Resolve 153

Chapter 8
PEACE 155

God's Command 157
Spring! 158
Rain 159
Anticipation 160
Raindrops 161
Boston Fern 162
Promise 163
Time 164
A Summer's Day 165
Dreamin' 166
Summer's Eve 167
Red Ribbons 168
Twilight 169
Night Lights 170
words 171
The Changing Moon 173
Moonlight 174
words 175
October Night 177
Silver Sliver 178
Passing of Time 179
First Snow 180
Winterland 181
Solace 182
Firelight 183
Awakening 184
Come Morning 185
Winter's Chill 186
Peace 187
Proverbs 3:13,17 189

Preface

When I was 8 years old I decided I wanted to become a teacher. It was also about that time that I fell in love with words. As a child, I spent hours reading, or writing and illustrating short stories, often forming them into small books.

A favorite memory is time spent sitting next to my grandfather, as he eloquently quoted poem after poem to me, while I listened with awe to words which seemed to flow effortlessly.

It was from those childhood experiences that I realized the beauty of the spoken word when recited in poetic form, and the power of the written word to express ideas.

I am, and have always been, an optimistic analyzer− a teacher and nurturer to all who would allow me.

After years of writing ideas in notebooks, and composing thoughts on napkins and small pieces of paper, it seemed time to gather it all together.

As I share these words with you, the reader, it is with the hope that they awaken a feeling, cause a new thought, or stir a past memory, while encouraging you to look more closely at that which surrounds you. And in doing so, may you find love, laughter, and peace…along the way.

Acknowledgments

My sincere and grateful appreciation go to Pat Brettnacher, Lois Palfi, and Ramona Wessel for their succinct editing, proofreading and helpful suggestions, and to Kristie Bender for her expertise with the final typesetting.

Also to Kim Shaffer whose kind and constant assurance helped an idea become a reality.

And most of all to my family and special friends, for their unconditional love, support, and willingness to listen again and again to thoughts and words in progress–always with enthusiasm and encouragement.

With love, I thank you all.

Trust in the Lord with all thine heart; and lean not unto thine own understanding. In all ways acknowledge him, and he shall direct thy paths.

Proverbs 3:5,6

Come Walk with Me

Come walk with me, along life's path,
  and share the moments as they pass.

Don't be afraid, or mourn what's passed,
  but drink of memories while they last.

A second can bring love and joy,
  or sadness, hurt, and grief–

Remember, though, as days go by
  a walk through life will travel fast.

So, take the time to feel and see–
    Come on…
        reflect…
            and walk with me.

Follow Me

Come walk with me
   and you will see
      the beauty here—

   Now I will lead…

Just follow me
   with open eyes
      and trust your heart—

I'll do my part
   to show you how
      to feel the peace—

   I'm here to lead…
      Just follow me!

And, behold, I am with thee, and will keep thee in all places whither thou goest ...

Genesis 28:15

To every thing there is a season,
and a time to every purpose under the heaven:
A time to be born, and a time to die;
A time to plant, and a time to pluck up
that which is planted;
A time to kill, and a time to heal;
A time to break down,
and a time to build up;
A time to weep, and a time to laugh;
A time to mourn, and a time to dance;
A time to cast away stones,
and a time to gather stones together;
A time to embrace,
and a time to refrain from embracing;
A time to get, and a time to lose;
A time to keep, and a time to cast away;
A time to rend, and a time to sew;
A time to keep silence, and a time to speak;
A time to love, and a time to hate;
A time of war, and a time of peace.

Ecclesiastes 3:1-8

To every thing there is a season, and a time to every purpose under heaven...

Ecclesiastes 3:1

-PURPOSE-

Dare to Be

Look, there!–among the hillside flowers,
   where flaming poppies grow.
So tall, and proud, and reaching high,
   to make their presence known.

Not bothered by, or caring if
   the other stems might bend,
Or paying much attention
   to the gently blowing wind.

But reaching on and stretching forth
   and daring to be bold,
Their colors loudly shouting
   the presence that they hold.

Reflect a bit, and wonder if,
   a lesson here is shown…
That we must stretch and dare to be,
   if we can ever grow!

Daybreak

Such a beautiful morning
    this quiet, hushed day.
Take time to reflect, and
    remember to pray–
For His guidance and love
    as you go on your way!

Awake!

A new day—
   Dawning.
      Open arms,
         Awake!

Misty,
   Moving,
      Mountainous Clouds.

         Ever changing
         Ever shaping...
            Days
            Lives.

Passing...
   Spreading life, across the horizon.

      Vibrant,
         Colors lighting the world.

            Giving direction
            Seeking...
               Showing the way.
                 Blessed!

Morning

The blazing sun peeks through the trees,
    and lights the morn for all to see.

As misty haze hangs over fields,
    while gentle breeze caresses leaves.

How many of us take this time
    to hope and plan and pray?

This quiet time we all could use,
    if only we would say:

"Good Morning, God,
    come with me now, as I begin my day…
I'll do my best, with every step,
    if You'll just lead the way!"

The Artist

The artist Himself
    paints the checkerboard skies,
Hues of crimsons and blues
    and grays fill our eyes.

Such breathtaking colors
    to light up our way,
And serve to remind us
    of His presence this day!

Sunset

Water Colors!

Royal Blue
Bold Purple
Vibrant Red

Spread across the sky, like a dashing cloak
furled around a young man's shoulders.

Dynamic end to another wondrous day!

    Reminders of moments,
      now gone forever.

        Time spent wisely—
           or squandered carelessly?

Reflections of the fading day slip…
    softly,
        slowly,
            silently,
                away.

That Eastern Light

So bright up in the eastern sky,
   surrounded by the dark.
A planet, or perhaps a star?
   We wonder what it is...

It shines alone, a beacon light,
   and with a magic presence gives
A special touch to early morn,
   before sun lights our way.

Though seldom seen, unveiled this day,
   perhaps to help us dream...
Of what may lie ahead of us
   and what our futures hold.
Unlike the rainbow sometimes shown—
   yet still, a glimpse of gold!

Extremes

My life's been touched by moments–
    extremes, the old folks say:
The hot of July desert,
    the frigid winter's day;
The wind of springtime's fury,
    the raging water's way;
But, oh, just give me presence
    of that, that's in between…

The warming rays of sun light,
    the cooling gentle rain;
The quiet springtime morning
    before the break of day;
The gentle falling leaves
    as autumn breezes sway;
The croaking of the bullfrogs
    round the stillness of the pond;
The lightly falling raindrops
    as they puddle on the ground;
The crispness of a summer breeze,
    the softly falling snow;
The crackle of the fireplace
    with its welcome, warming glow.

Yes, I, I'll choose the middle path,
  the one that lets me know...

The softer times,
  the gentle ways of life's amazing days.
No raging sides, no judgment stands,
  or cause for just *one* man,
But welcoming, and open hearts
  and love that can transform;
And tolerance, and patience shown
  and joys that can be known!

So, I, I'll take that middle road,
  the one with peaceful ways...
And leave the edges of extremes
  for yet another day!

Landmark

The sycamore stands so tall and straight,
    a landmark showing nature's gate.
Beyond such place where one can find
    a rippling brook, or water's kind.

A beacon when confused or lost,
    a way to lead, or quench our thirst.
The only thing we need to know?–
    to lift our eyes so God can show!

The Mighty Oak

The great white oak within the wood,
   a mighty presence known,
With twisted limbs and bended trunk,
   its strength is proudly shown.

A pillar there, against blue sky,
   a landmark of all time,
Its knowledge of the days gone by
   holds memories of mankind.

The wonders it could share with us
   if it could tell the tales–
Of days and deeds and men and feats
   of times so long ago...

Perhaps we then would solve the quest,
   and truths at last we'd know!

"Things do not change; we change."

-Henry David Thoreau-

A time to be born, and a time to die…

Ecclesiastes 3:2

- LIFE -

2

Sharing

A midwife's hands,
  holding
    helping
      guiding
        praying.

A midwife's heart,
  loving
    giving
      sharing
        healing.

A gentle touch,
A warm embrace,
An encouraging nod,
A spoken word...
All given with unselfish love.

A brief meeting,
  An intimate sharing,
    A special time,
      A lasting friendship.

A Miracle

CHANGES...
    Excitement.
    Can it soon be?
    Sleepy, tired body.
    Tears, mixed with joy.
    Morning, noon, and night sickness.
        Is there *really* someone?

        Elation!
        Movement!
        Roller-coaster butterflies.
        Blessed is this sacred, life-giving body.
        Thanks be to God!

GROWTH...
    Each day a new experience.
    Renewed strength, anticipation.
    Daily changes, changing profile–
    Is this body mine?
    Who shares from within?

        Dreams!
        X-rated, comedies, mysteries,
        Interrupted, yet continuing on.
        Restless mind, and tired body,
        Awake to each new day–
        Night memories left behind.
        Rejoice!
        Anticipate!

HEAVINESS...
　Awkward, cumbersome, beautiful body!
　Turtle-like movements, cracks and groans.
　Surrender to that unyielding, unknown,
　Force within.

　　　Uncertainties!
　　　Fear and excitement.
　　　Bold, bouncing baby,
　　　Making your presence known.
　　　　　Changes...nothing is ever the same.

A CHOSEN DAY...
　Mystical, serene, reverent.
　The moon? The tides?
　A special pact with God?
　Hush!...watch.

　　　A new life begins.
　　　An old life is changed.
　　　Eyes of wonder greet a new world.
　　　Eyes of love greet a new being.

LIFE...
　Ups and downs.
　Moving on and growing old.
　Profound wisdoms and gentle thoughts
　All—
　　　Revert back to one solitary,
　　　Sacred, moment of greeting...

　　　　　　　　　　　　BIRTH

Child

My child...

Open
  Loving
    Innocent

Rambunctious
  Rowdy
    Alive!

Meeting life
  Challenging
    Trusting

GROW!

Claire

This is the night that my baby girl died,
    deep in my womb…before first daylight.
Unaware yet was I
    so no tears had I cried,
For instead I believed
    she'd soon be at my side.

But sometimes things don't go
    as we'd wished or we'd planned,
And our hearts question "Why?"
    at God's powerful hands.

Though we may *never* have answers
    to "why's" or "what if's,"
We *always* can count on the one promised gift…
The love from our Father
    as He guides us through life,
In darkness and sadness,
    and sorrow and strife.

So, I choose to remember
    from years long since past,
And I let myself feel
    all the love my heart has.
Still not knowing the reason
    she can't be with me,
I hold on to her memory
    and to things which won't be.

One Solitary Rose

ONE SOLITARY ROSE...
    In deepest shade of red,
        given by her brother in the solemn, after birth.

TEARS from heaven rain...
    As a two gun salute breaks the quiet–
        reminding of the two days she's been gone.

TIME stands still in the hushed mourning cemetery.
    The place is chosen, the earth awaits.

        One solitary rose...
            placed at her heart in cloth,
        A lasting remembrance
            of one pressed between pages.

        One blue dress...
            covered with white hearts,
        Pure in spirit, telling of spoken love
            she'll never hear.

ONE SOLITARY ROSE...
    Soft, velvet petals,
        like the touch of her sweet lips–
    Never to utter a word,
        yet speaking to our hearts forever.

The Opened Gift

Bright lights shining on the tree
Mistletoe and popcorn strung,
Gaily wrapped presents of red and green
Peppermint sticks and Christmas cheer,
Busy shoppers, falling snow,
"Christmas Eve quiet" and candlelit tea…

> The story's told.
> The Christ child lives.
> Our savior's born.

Behold, a dream…
> A beautiful child dances round the tree,
> excitement in her eyes.
> *An unopened gift.*

REPEATS…the scene in our Father's home.

> Joy and laughter…with Lordly hosts.
> The girl dances…with angel's wings.
> The music plays…in heavenly tunes.
> The gifts abound…in grace and love.

> The quiet eve…a reverent time.
> *An opened gift, to God.*

Love Lost

How wrong our lives can sometimes be,
   when loved ones we have lost...

We know not why, or how to see
   the reasons we are tossed–

      into that place of emptiness
      where questions that we hold,
      and answers that our hearts cry out for,
      often go untold.

One minute more, a day gone by,
   heart's heaviness still lasts.

We wonder if we *ever* can move on,
   beyond the past...

But move we shall, for time plays on,
    while memories we'll hold dear–
Reliving all those precious gifts
    as days turn into years…

Each lifetime smile, and hug, and tear,
    remembered through the grief–
With heartfelt love and sadness
    in every step we take.

Until that day, when we can see
    the light beyond the clouds…

And trust, once more, in God to bring
    a joy back in our soul–
So we can help the others
    when their story, too, is told.

Silver-hair Lady

That silver-hair lady
    who exudes grace and charm,
Sends expressions of love
    wrapped within her soft arms.

While glimpses of thoughts
    from the years long ago,
Bring memories to mind
    of the joys she has known.

But the pillar of strength
    that we've known in our past,
Seems no longer here—
    by *her* choice, now at last.

And each precious moment
    just seems to rush by,
As we helplessly watch her
    resolution to die.

Mother's Love

There's nothing like a mother's love,
  or softness of her touch,
To calm our fears, and dry our tears
  and comfort us so much.

The fresh baked cookies after school,
  and welcomed "Come home!" call at noon...

Those childhood days we spent with her
  recalled with love and praise–
When time has passed, and she is gone,
  our memories never fade!

Gray Morning

Gray, quiet morning.
Saddened stillness.
Soft, private tears.
Another mother has left our earth…
Trod gently on our broken hearts.

Our unconditional, all loving, giving,
    source of support has gone.
Wrap Your arms around us God,
    for we are frightened and alone.

Somewhere–Somewhere…
The sounds of sweet harmony drift–
Smiles and laughter of loved ones sharing,
Void of all suffering, sorrow, and pain.
Remember…Rejoice…

The starlit darkness will close this day,
    and the sun will rise in the morn.
Let the heavens open to receive one precious mom!

The Visit

A sadness felt deep in our soul,
   the loss so hard to bear,
So we return occasionally
   to a private place that's there…

Between the stones, upon the hill,
   no others are around,
With blanket spread, we think awhile
   and sit upon the ground.

That place, wherein our loved ones lie,
   our worlds so far apart,
But knowing, while we sit near them,
   we're close within our heart.

We stay not long…an hour or two
   to cry and reminisce,
And then move on to meet our day
   just leaving one last kiss.

"Grief returns with the revolving year."

-Percy Bysshe Shelley-

A time to plant, and a time to pluck up that which is planted...

Ecclesiastes 3:2

-SEASONS-

3

Cycles

A beginning of ends...
An end of familiar.
 What was, is no more;
 What is, yet unknown;
 What will be–still to come!

A time for each season,
So states the Good Book.
 A time we must cry,
 And a time to rejoice.
 A time to stay quiet,
 And a time we must voice.

Our part not to worry,
Or question, or choose...
But to let each day guide us
Down paths we are shown–
 To futures uncertain,
 In times that will come.

The Place

    Silent,
    Peaceful
    Privacy.

A time for reflection…
    sorting ideas and beliefs.

Dealing with life
    frightening, yet necessary.

Far from crowds,
    away from people.

A place of reckoning…

    The Farmer's Field.

Solitude

One solitary cornfield
  a gentle rain
  stillness.

Tractors in the distance
  soft roar
  muffled birds.

Time is motionless.

The Man

    tender
    gentle

Beneath his suit of duty

    meeting…
        facing life's challenges
          following
            turning
              choosing
                correcting

Each year different from the last

    reflecting past
        experiencing present
          anticipating future
            growing
              and causing growth…

    dedicated
      strong
        ongoing
            ever-changing, sameness.

Land bought, land sold
more farming, less farming
lack of control.

God-like landlords
plowing begun, plowing done
maybe tomorrow,
maybe next year?

Change
Courage...
SILENT COURAGE

waiting
hoping
praying
watching
reaping

never-ending cycle
never-ending gamble.

The Farmer.

A Witness

Corn standing tall

witnessing to God

alone…

questioning
searching
reaching
grasping
wonder.

Rejuvenated strength in the
quiet of day.

Picking Corn

Rows and rows

   standing tall

     reaching…

Slicing through

   squashing

  spitting out

   heaping

 piles of corn.

Bringing in the Crops

Trucks in single file
   in the mist of morning–
      waiting for the last topping of fill.

Slowly moving
Cautiously as a turtle–
   churning
    turning
     grinding
      straining
       roaring
         gaining speed
           turning corners
              ever so carefully…

Single file–
   waiting for their turn to empty.

Beds raising slowly,
   beans and corn
      raining...

Disappearing into that mysterious,
   deep, black hole.

     smiles
     chatter
     light-hearted
     swift-moving
     on-going
     repeating,

     TRUCKS.

Harvest

Trucks piled...lined
like children in a hallway
waiting for drinks.

Taking turns–
sometimes patiently,
sometimes not.

Hurry!
time moves
weather watches.

Breakdowns–
nerves tensed...

Farmers wait.

The Job

Coffee cups
Laughter
Comradeship

      Beans
      Corn prices
      Questionable futures

The binding force...
Silent
Secretive, yet powerful.

Lives entwined,
Unspoken truths.

      Parting of ways–

Trucks dumping...
Only to return again.

The Season

The era ends
The season is over
Tractors change color
   with the surrounding landscape.

     Tearing
     Gnawing
Pulling out that which has been
   meticulously planted.

     Change is due,
     Needed…

What was–is no more
What will be–will.

Tomorrow comes…
The cycle continues,
   yet stays the same.

     Changing
     Repeating
     Cycle of life…

     WELCOME!

*A time to break down,
and a time to build up...*

Ecclesiastes 3:3

-PROMISE-

4

*When prayers are sent...
blessings return!*

Blessings

Waken to the splendor
   of the early morning sun,
And let your spirit fill
   with the new day that's begun.

Lift your face toward Heaven
   to thank the Lord, first thing,
And plan your daily chores
   while counting each blessing!

Moment of Truth

Mystical splendor,
    blankets a serene and hushed world…

Alas, the first light of morn
    awakens a new day with
        whispers of anticipation.

CELEBRATE…the world comes alive!

    Waste not a single second
        in worry of what is–
            or what might be.

HASTEN…to embrace each unfolding
    moment of truth.

        A day awaits!

The Unveiling

Gray misty day.
 Gently falling rain
  tapping rhythms of the heart.

So much to contemplate,
 discover...
When the mist rises
 and day is seen again in sunlit beauty,
What then?
What will be unveiled in the fresh awakening?

Hold fast to the peacefulness of the moment,
 the quiet falling drops.
Find rest in the presence of time
 reflect, remember...

Embrace each of life's faces.
Soon, *very soon*, change will come again!

Life's River

Rolling river, gliding by,
   like swiftly moving time.
Moment's memories swept away,
   along with changing currents.

A thought, an instant, etched in mind—
   while time and days move on…
Sometimes fast, and sometimes slow,
   yet, ever flowing on.

We cannot fight the current
   that changes every day,
But we can flow with peace and hope
   along our river's way.

And trust, believe, embrace,
   what each day soon may send—
For we will never know
   what lies around the bend!

Though clouds of life may at times
look dark and ominous, beneath each cloud
is a silver lining of an angel's wing
gently hovering…
   Close enough to protect us,
      and keep us in God's light.

Angels

Never for an instant doubt that angels are around—
Just because we cannot see them
or can't hear their sounds.

Sometimes we can not explain
all that surrounds us,
But often we're reminded
by a simple touch...

That they have never left our side,
and we should trust as much!

Gentle Souls

Upon our earth walk gentle souls
    who dignify mankind.
Their purpose comes from deep within,
    their gestures soon remind–

How kindness, truth and love for all
    flow forth from them each day,
To touch a life, or warm a heart,
    or brighten someone's way…

The man who gives his shirt away
    to him whose need is great,
The friend who listens with her heart
    until the hour is late.
The one who works the long, hard hours
    until his back is tired,
To earn a wage to clothe and feed
    his wife and little child.

The healing kiss, the warm embrace
    within a mother's arms–
Encouragement, belief and trust
    that shelter us from harm.
The sister and the brother,
    the friend and preacher-man,
The neighbor and the lover
    all there to lend a hand.

So many steps within our lives
    and paths to choose or cross–
What special folk God places here
    so we are never lost!

A privilege we are sometimes shown
    when one may come our way,
To touch our hearts and fill our lives
    with all they do and say.

New Year's Eve

The eve of New Year is fading fast
    as firelight flames dance high,
Outside the moon is hanging low
    and stars fill up the sky.

A time to think, and reminisce
    of all that's past this year—
Of joys and days and happenings
    and all those we hold dear.

We're sad to see the old year end,
    the happy times we've known,
But ready now, to forge ahead
    to future paths we're shown!

And like the moon that floats tonight—
  ink-black with silvered edge,
Our thoughts turn to a future time
  and what might lie ahead...

With darkness in our questioned minds,
  no certainties or paths,
We'll try to take each tiny step
  as if it were our last—

And keep that image of the moon,
  it's silver edge exposed,
As promise for the days to come—
  of times we are to know.

A New Day

Just as surely as a river runs,
    time itself began…
Like pages turning one by one–
Each memory adding chapters
    until the book is done.
The rushing of each single stream,
    the ebb and flow of tides,
The future days of years to come,
    the life that's passed us by.

Such precious time and private thoughts
    of heart's desires–love lost and found,
The circling of the moon and stars,
    life's cycles here on ground.

The minutes tick…
Our hearts beat fast,
    our lives an endless rush.
Yet, somewhere…there, within the soul,
    there lies the deepest sense–
Of love, true love, and answers known
    to mysteries that life has shown.

Dare we, just once, allow ourselves
    to live what life could be,
And truly know what God can give
    to meet our every need?

Perhaps we should, this New Year's Day,
    a single moment spare,
To take the time to feel, reflect,
    and dream a moment where...
We strive to see what lies ahead
    if only we will dare–

To listen once with all our heart
    to what our God has taught.
Believe, go forth, each moment trust
    what always is unknown–
Have peace, dare more, show courage
    (often not displayed),
And make tomorrow more
    than just a start of any day!

Reach out, in love, with open hearts,
    hold back no more this year–
For we cannot know complete love
    until we lose our fears!

The year begins on this day one,
    full of hope and love...
Anticipate life's ebbs and flows,
    but turn your eyes toward God!

A time to keep, and a time to cast away...

Ecclesiastes 3:6

-MEMORIES-

5

Slowly passing clouds,
  like swirling cotton candy,
Dissipating shapes and forms
  hold memories from the past...

First Day

Chalk dust and pencils,
    and new books, bound tight.
Crisp clothes and haircuts,
    remember the sight?

Excitement and nerves
    greet each friend that they meet–
New teachers, new class rules,
    new faces, new seats.

New places and schedules
    and memories to keep…
A first day behind them,
    which soon they'll repeat!

Sleepless

Strange, deep noises in the night,
   cracks and pops before daylight.

Eerie voices, weird-like tunes,
   morning can't arrive too soon!

   Close my eyes, and plug my ears,
   Pull the blankets overhead.
   Scared? Not me, I don't believe in—
   Spooks and ghosts…I'm safe in bed.

There!…just then,
   is that some sunlight
   gently rising through the dew?

Good, although I'm not afraid now,
   light does give a different view!

May Day Violets

Along the path where violets grow,
   I'll stoop to pick just one or two–
And gently brush the morning dew
   from top their soft, soft petals.

And close my eyes, and sweetness smell
   and take a second to decide…
And plan to whom I'll bring surprise.

With nothing but a small bouquet
   I'll tiptoe 'round their house,
And ring the bell, and leave it there,
   as quiet as a mouse.

For one small gift can spirits lift,
   so early on this day,
And with it bring some heartfelt joy,
   before I'm on my way!

August Baseball

The hot, muggy air
   hangs so thick all around,
While moths circle lights
   high above the damp ground.

And the clicking of cleats
   strike a rhythmic chord,
To the swing of the bats
   and the crowd's muffled roar.

A sea full of numbers,
   of colors and dust,
The umpire's loud calls
   and the outs to discuss.

The crack of the ball
   from the bat to the glove,
Heard again and again
   in the game that they love.

A hot summer evening,
   plays late into night,
Popcorn and ice cream
   a commonplace sight.

Those nights to remember,
   some day long from then…
When moments and memories
   are relived once again!

Trail Ride

When the sound of the hooves
    strike the hard, dusty trail...
And the swishing of tail,
    and the gentle swayed gait
Cause the saddle to groan
    and to creak and to strain–

It's then I'm reminded
    of the power felt beneath,
And the union of trust
    that man shares with his beast!

Tranquillity

Intricate spider webs
   hang from the limbs,
And the first touch of fall
   shows in colors it sends.

A swishing of tail,
   and a whinny of horse,
   (while hooves clank on rocks
   as we splash down the creek),
Give a serene feeling…
   just the presence I need!

The Clearing

Blue skies all around us
   with white cotton clouds,
   frame the first of fall colors–
   while highlights of red
   kiss the tips of the leaves,
   before drifting down gently
   to rest in the creek.

There's a splash felt below us
   when hooves strike the rocks,
   so we stop just a moment
   in this cool, clearing place–
   while fish swim beneath us,
   and shade covers our faces.

Again then we start
   when the horses have drunk,
   up the trail, through the woods–
   taking care to dodge limbs
   as we climb the small bank.

'Till at last when we come
   to the opening we see,
   and step out in the clearing
   surrounded by trees.

Where the warmth of the day
   touches our faces and souls,
   and the beauty surrounds us
   while moments unfold...

A field full of golden rod,
   bees buzzing round,
   Queen Anne's lace, and daisies
   with centers of black,
   cabbage butterflies, monarchs,
   and the sun on our backs.

While clouds gently drift
   overhead as we sit...
   so still without motion
   we riders give rein,
   letting horses taste sweet clover
   while chomping their bits.

And although we would love
to remain here so long,
the time soon comes
when we must move on.

So with thoughts locked inside
of our hearts and our minds,
we ride on down the trail
to the place where we find...

At last we must end
this perfect time spent,
and return to the place
of our jobs and our friends.

It's a day filled with memories
and a horse that we shared...
a time of camaraderie,
friendship and care.

In the Barn

The patter of drops
    upon the tin roof,
The sweet smell of hay
    from the loft high above,
Awaken the memories
    from days long since past...

When we lay on our backs
    and all time stood still,
And we listened to rain
    while our senses were filled—
    with the smell of the leather
    and dampness of earth,
    the neigh of a horse
    and a soft breeze or two.

If we close our eyes tightly
    and let ourselves dream,
We can almost still hear
    that soft patter of rain.

Village Blacksmith

A small crack in the door
   lets a stream of sun through,
And casts shadows of light
   on the fresh morning dew.

While the clanging of sounds
   send sweet symphonies of noise,
And the pounding of metal
   drowns out any voice.

There is sweat on his brow
   and a hot smell of coals,
As the hiss and the steam
   help to shape the right mold.

The blacksmith's own rhythm
   heard again and again…

As neighs come from horses
   who wait for their turn,
And the touch of the hands
   that are callused and learned.

The Town Jeweler

As he peered through his loupe,
    his back slightly bent,
Arms stiffened and still,
    his gaze stayed intent.
He knew what to look for
    seeing each minute thing–
Taking note of the size,
    shape, and color of ring.

He had years of gained knowledge
    of diamonds and gold,
Of rubies, and sapphires,
    and emeralds he'd sold.

But the time passed on by,
    and the years brought–progress?
Chain stores in malls
    and computers on-line,
Took us far, far away
    from that once-upon-time…

When he peered through his loupe
 as he gazed with intent,
Filled with knowledge and answers
 and wisdom he'd lent–
To hundreds of folks
 during years that he'd spent
As the town's trusted jeweler,
 and respected old friend.

A gift of himself
 and of service, so rare–
A memory of time
 sadly missed on townsquare.

The Carpenters

The tools of the trade
    though not many, enough,
    most of which fit
    in a belt or a box.

Just a level, a square,
    a hammer, some nails,
    a tape, and a plumb,
    and a saw and a drill.

Each used with such care
    and exactness of thought—
    with preciseness of measure
    and patience untouched.

Our father and Father
    both build with their hands,
    and fruits of their labor
    changed the direction of man.

Behold…
 The wonder of Christmas
  within a child's eyes,
  And sparkle of tree-lights
  that light up our lives!

Dream Lights

Gaze deep into the bubble lights
    that decorate the tree–
And dream of wishes and of hope,
    and things you'd like to see.

Reflect a while on years gone by,
    and futures yet to be…
And where your time has most been spent,
    and where new paths may lead.

For all it takes is just one thought
    to bring your heart alive–
And give you hope and make you feel
    just like those shining lights!

Christmas

Such joy and excitement
    within a child's soul–
The true meaning of Christmas,
    when Christ's story is told!

The heralds of angels
    with voice ringing high–
While friends greet old friends,
    as they pass by.

This splendor of season
    comes but once a year–
And touches each heart,
    both far and near.

It brings with it laughter,
    fond memories held dear–
But most of all...
    magic to last through the year!

Christmas Morn

Strands of lights upon the tree.
Brightly colored packages,
   gifts soon to see!

Child-delight wonder,
   hearts filled with joy.
Happiness wishes…
   for each girl and boy!

Fir

branches holding

brightly glowing lights

angel watching from above

popcorn and cranberry garlands

shiny colored presents stacked with love

wonder and excitement in a child's eyes

Christmas is coming

soon!

déjà vu

These roads I traveled as a child,
   I thought I'd left behind...
But here I am, again this day,
   in yet another time.

The big oak tree still looks the same,
   although the street has changed—
Some houses gone, some new ones built,
   some landmarks still remain.

I thought I'd never come this way
   again in my life's days,
But I should never think I know,
   or even try to guess...

Just when I think I'm far beyond,
   I'm right back in my past!

Neither words nor time can be recalled...

A time to keep silence, and a time to speak...

Ecclesiastes 3:7

-QUESTIONS-

6

Backwards

A backwards day,
A backwards day,
   So that is what this is!

A task is done, and then one more,
   each goal is met today.

So smooth the time it passes
   as we go on our way.

But then…oh my, what is this thing?
   this backwards awful thing–
That takes those tasks that we have done,
   and wrecks them one by one.

Until which time we wonder if
   they ever were complete,
Or just a wishful thought of ours
   that soon we must repeat!

Restless Hearts

What makes us want to seek and search
   for more than we have now?

Our restless hearts and thoughts, we find,
   cause questions in our minds!

Could it soon be...
   by chance *or* choice—
   when hearts cry out, we'll hear some voice?

And then we'll know...
   when flames still dance, and embers burn—
   the things we'll do, the ways we'll turn?

Questions

Where am I going?
Where have I been?

   "That is what life's all about, my friend."

What will I do now?
What should I have done?
Is it time now to walk, or maybe to run?

What lies ahead there,
Beyond tomorrow's door–
Sadness and sorrow,
Love, laughter, or more?

   "Life's but a moment that's hardly begun…
   Those questions you'll have,
   'Till your earth's steps are done."

It is a necessary part of life
to gain knowledge by questioning
"what-ifs, and wherefores"...

But wherever we search,
whatever we seek—God is with us,
to catch us when we fall, or lead us
when we've gone astray.

His presence is certain,
His love, steadfast.

Fools

The world is full of fools to see—
   by choice they choose to be!
Their actions and their mishaps,
   displayed in every deed.

Like rats within a maze
   they bump from side to side,
Not caring where they're heading
   or why they are alive.

Their eyes so blindly viewing
   the world that is about,
The choices they are making
   determine foolish routes.

One wonders if they ever are
   to see beyond their face,
And choose some greater knowledge
   than what lies within their maze!

The Lonely Man

Away he goes,
    eyes straight ahead–
With shoulders bowed,
    and feelings dead.

Afraid is he,
    of all who would–
Come close and love him,
    if they could.

With armor up
    around his soul,
He walks alone
    with heart that's cold.

He gazes left,
    and then to right–
Then saunters off into the night.

What If?

We often sit and contemplate
   the days and years gone by–
And wonder what we're soon to find,
   or what ahead will lie.

If one were sure of times to come,
   what then? what if? would he?...
Reach out...to step, to try, to gaze
   at futures yet to be?

Stardust

Have you ever watched the stardust
    as it floats from up above,
And wondered where the ceiling
    of Heaven really was?

Or gazed at autumn leaves
    as they gently fall to ground,
To blanket nature's surface
    barely making any sound?

Have you taken but a second
    to smell the fresh spring rain,
Or thought of golden wheat
    as it blows across the plain?

Our days are filled, our lives pass by,
    our memories linger on,
While moments come, and moments go,
    there are things we wished we'd done.

If we could now, one minute more,
    relive just one small part…
The things we'd do, and say, or be
    are captured in our heart!

The twinkling of stars,
　　as we look down from this thing…
Shows an up-side-down world
　　beneath the airplane's wing!

Heaven's Sunset

A sunset there, *on top* the clouds,
so close to heaven's face!
Where only angels pause to rest
away from hectic pace.

A sharing of that secret place
where perfect stillness keeps—
Like freshly falling snow,
or water ripples stilled
(we've known from times below).

Our hearts reflect,
Our souls are touched,
What is this special thing…

That we can only know or see
above the airplane's wing?

The Flight

Floating on a sea of clouds,
   distant views of flat plateaus—

We *must* be the near the keeper's gate
   where angels' wings reflect the sun!

   Why are we here?
   How can we dare
      to bridge the gap so close?

   One moment more,
   A stolen glimpse…
      of beauty yet unknown.

Airplane's View

The sunset fades,
  the sky turns gray
  and stillness overcomes.

Soft hush of angels' whispers
  soon tell that day is done.

But wait!
There off–a distant light,
  a sparkle breaks the dark...

A glimmer of a promise kept,
  shines upward from the ground.

If I could fly
above the trees,
and choose the things
I'd like to be…

I think I'd fly
around and 'round,
at last to choose
what's here on ground!

My Secret

There's a place in the woods
that I go to sometimes–
Far removed from all else,
framed by only sunshine.

It's a private, found site
and few are aware–
Of my best kept secret,
which seldom I share.

A place quiet for thoughts
where I dream and I plan–
A spot surely like heaven
but here, on my land.

This one special place
where I play and I pray,
Far removed from all else
that fills up my day!

A Place

Feeling wind on my face
    and sun in my eyes,
I jog the pace of a runner's life.

Each moment passing
    like clouds rushing by,
Away from the burdens
    that my day can know—
To a place in my mind
    where only *I* go.

Where the beat of my footsteps
    on concrete will bring...
That solitude feeling I get as I run—
That peace in my soul
    that I share with no one!

Escape

While he jogs just for fun—
   from life's lessons he runs.

And the tears on his cheek
   hide from all those he meets...

As he jogs ever on—
   until *those* thoughts are gone!

"I would rather sit on a pumpkin, and have it all to myself, than to be crowded on a velvet cushion."

-Henry David Thoreau-

A time to love, and a time to hate...

Ecclesiastes 3:8

-LOVE-

7

Sounds of Love

Just listen to the rain
    as it gently falls our way,
A cleansing of the heavens
    on this peaceful, springtime day.

The chirping of the distant birds,
    the call of lonesome dove,
The caws of blackbirds passing by…
    all sounds of quiet love!

Gold

The end of the rainbow
    lies within my lover's eyes,
The greenest lush of meadows
    and deepest blue of skies.

The promise of dreams shared
    between our two souls–
The hopes and desires
    that each one of us holds.

A mirror to the other
    two hearts joining fast,
Both throbbing with feelings
    unknown from the past!

Lovers' Moon

Bright October moon
   suspended in the sky,
Lighting paths and searching hearts
   as lovers watch with eyes…

Full of hope and promises
   as their lives entwine,
Sharing hugs and new found love,
   and dreams of future times.

A Gift

A crackling fire with reddened glow
   (to help make memories as time flows)
And shimmering candles' dancing lights,
   while fresh white snow reflects moonlight...

Plus something special, sheer black lace
   and fluted stemware—wine on ice,
Softly playing Christmas tunes,
   and colored tree-lights lightened room.

My wish for you?...
Someone to hold—
   to talk, to laugh, to kiss,
   to cuddle with, and share and dance,
   and keep the moments with.
I can't think of a better thing
   than giving such a gift!

Love

Sometimes love just passes by,
   sometimes it will stay.
Sometimes love is side by side,
   moving through each day.

But *sometimes* love is intertwined
   two souls each joining fast,
One giving to the next
   what the other lacks.
Holding on, and growing with
   every heart's desire,
Giving, helping, sharing,
   stoking…each the other's fire.

Life shows love of every kind
   as we walk our paths,
But few will know the latter—
   or a love that lasts!

A Kiss

A kiss is such a precious thing,
    a gift of love to share–
A tender touch, a warm embrace
    to tell someone you care.

Unlike the one you'd give a friend,
    your sister or your mother,
The lover's kiss, a special kind,
    shows passion for another.

It means so much, with loving kiss,
    to stroke and hold each other–
Don't let a single day go by
    without kissing your lover!

For days move on and weeks are gone
    and time so quickly passes,
And yet, there is just one small thing
    to make sure love will last…

A single kiss can mean so much
    when freely it is given–
Not stol'n, or begged, or nightly planned,
    or used to make amends!

If we were only half aware
    of what a kiss can tell,
We'd *always* start and end each day
    with one to keep love well.

We'd know that if a love were true
    we'd never need to ask–
For sharing of that single kiss
    would make sure feelings last!

The Missing Part

The day goes by, and then one more—
    a kiss is never spent,
And feelings that he holds inside,
    too bad, are never sent.

A little thing, a kiss should be,
    to thank, or love, or share—
A tender feeling, thought, or deed
    to make someone aware…

That love holds fast and feelings last,
    (although they're seldom told),
Yet nonetheless the heart would know
    that love had not grown cold!

But none is sent, this day or next,
    a sadly missing part…
So time moves on, and days add to
    a sadness in the heart.

"Hope"

Like gentle raindrops on the pane
    her tears so softly fall,
For what once was, and what is now,
    and what she never saw.

    But one can dream...

And dream she does...forever holding tight
    to feelings that she *hopes* will come,
    to promises that might.

But first, this time of sad regret
    will have its place in heart,
Where she will bide the time, and wait
    until tomorrow's start–

    When life plays out...

    Each moment shown,
    Like actors in a part.

Love Thoughts

We have...Two eyes to see it all,
        Two ears to hear a call,
        Two hands to hold a loved one,
and a heart with...
        Two chambered walls.

Would it not then be possible
To look with loving eyes,
And hear love's spoken words, and such–

        But...
        Instead of just with one true love,
        Embrace love *Twice* as much?

Divided Heart

Two chambers, so the heart doth have,
    a left one and a right–
Each filled with special substance
    and presence to give life.

From hence there comes a powerful love
    to share with someone found,
Whose traits and soul and qualities
    are unlike those around.

But herein lies a paradox,
    which often goes untouched...
The chance there is for one to love
    from *both* sides–just as much!

And if a second love is known,
    a rich life it would be–
For many of us never find
    that first love which we need!

Questioned Love

In dancing flames...
    a heart doth see
        beneath the sheltered gaze,

        a fond embrace
        a moment held
        in thoughts of distant days.

A heart doth tell...
    of memories past
        of tears and love and need,

        of sharing souls
        and private words
        and special meaning deeds.

Who *is* that one, that certain one,
    with whom we dare to share–
Our innermost of private selves,
    our views, our thoughts, our prayers?

A special one, that him or her,
    that one we let so close...

A forward step, and then two back,
    such cautious moves we make–
We question feelings deep inside
    not wanting to partake!

    Our hearts cry out.
    We wonder why.
    We do not need this love!

Yet...are we ever *really* sure
    who's sent from God to love?

The Runner's Soul

With the wind at his back
   and the sweat on his brow,
His beating chest pounds
   while his feet drum a sound–
With a cadence of beat
   as the rhythm repeats…

And the sound of his heart
   reminds him some way,
Of the passing of time
   as he jogs on this day.

The world travels by
   as the sun lights the sky,
And he tries to find
   in this moment of time–
That faraway place
   where no thoughts taunt his mind.

That one special place
   that's so far from all else,
Where the pain in his heart
   and the tear in his eye,
Won't be noticed by those
   who would ask and then know…
Of his innermost thoughts
   and the truth of his soul!

That one private place,
    where at last he can dare–
To open his heart
    and to himself bare…

The most secret feelings
    he keeps locked within–
Never daring to feel,
    or to show, or to send.

So protected is he
    from those who would care…
If he'd only decide
    to acknowledge and share–
Perhaps then he may find
    just how some do believe
In the runner's *true* self,
    and the love that he needs.

But…until that day comes
    when he chooses to know,
He'll continue to run
    in the wind and the sun–
Never daring to see, or to take, or to ask,
    from those who may offer the things which he lacks.

This special time kept, a renewing of soul…
    his place to escape, to revere, and to grow.

Safe

So, faster and faster and faster he runs…

Each breath keeping time
    as his heart starts to drum.
'Till the thoughts in his mind
    seem far, far away,
And the pain in his heart
    is numbed by the sound,
Of the rhythm of footsteps
    that strike the hard ground.

Each moment and heartbeat,
    reminders of time…
As he runs in the sleet, snow
    and morning sunshine.
His time to release
    all the heartaches of day–
His time to find peace,
    in the runner's own way.

Will he ever slow down,
   or face up to his thoughts?
Will he miss what life shows,
   or what could be taught?
Will he choose not to feel—
   what is there, or might be?
Will he close his eyes tightly
   afraid that he'll see?

So protected he feels,
   from the world and himself,
When he jogs down that path
   as he starts each new day...
Never quite facing facts
   or wanting to see—
What's right there before him,
   or could possibly be!

So he continues to run
   to that place deep within—
Where he hides from the truth,
   from himself, and from friends.

A Race

He runs until *his* race is done—
    I wonder what he's running from?
In coolness of the quiet morn,
    a day softly begins...

The runner's own world,
    where a soul's deepest thoughts
    are allowed to be free—
If for only those moments
    when no one can see.

With a breeze on his cheek
    and the hint of a tear,
He relaxes his guard
    while no one is near...

His mind races on,
    and his steps follow true.
Is he running from love,
    or is it on his mind, too?

One Moment

A gaze of eyes
A brush of lips
A touch of souls
A link of hearts.

Each challenging the other
　　to speak
That which must go unspoken–
　at least for now
　at least for now.

Impasse

Nose to nose, and breath to breath,
    heart to heart... afraid to start.
Today no further will they go,
    tomorrow will bring, what no one knows.
A wrestling match 'tween heart and head,
    with feelings now aroused, thought dead!

And if they dare, one single time,
    to feel at first with heart,
Would second love find courage then
    to share the other's part?

When both have always followed mind...
    what if a greater love they'd find,
If once they were to follow blind
    with only feelings of the kind—
That others they have known have felt
    when similar choices they've been dealt?

Or would they find, because of fear,
    they'd have to turn from love so near?
And though they'd cling to spoken words
    (though false pretenses said),
They'd seem confused and question why
    down certain paths they're lead...
And wonder were there stepping stones
    to greater love ahead?

But if a lesson they're to learn...
　　it's put their trust in God,
For He will plan the steps they take
　　and challenge errors made
(Though often what they most desire
　　will somehow find its way).

And so, today they fight a change
　　from anything now known,
Yet, in due time, when things are right
　　some new way they'll be shown.

For often when there is a need
　　to shift a path we start,
We have to learn to still our minds
　　and listen with our hearts!

Silver Vase

A single rose.
A silver vase.
Unspoken love behind the face.

A fragile heart about to break.
A single rose.
A silver vase.

Infidelity

The poison in my inner core
Might someday raise its head, once more…

Not knowing *if* to trust
or when
I dare not show my love again!

Timing

A friend once called it timing,
    life's happenstance and chance—
That thing that takes an answer
    and questions it instead!

The hows and whys our lives unfold
    in such the way they do,
As we are left to wonder
    if others question, too.

If we could change one single thing
    about our lives today…
What would we be, or do, or say
    to shift our life's pathway?

Resolve

Dancing flames, soothing notes,
   background music,
     as memories float.

Reddened embers, glowing lights,
   laughter heard,
     throughout the night.

Questioning minds
   ask what is to come?
Sending prayers high above,
   wishful thinking is done…

Stare into the coals,
   while attempting to see–
Then return with resolve
   to that which will be.

A time of war, and a time of peace...

Ecclesiastes 3:8

-PEACE-

8

God's Command

The fury of lightening
   in God's flashing eyes,
The roar of the thunder
   that fills up the sky.
The torrents of raindrops
   that plummet to land…
All serve to remind us of
   God's powerful hand!

The rage of the wind
   and the crack of the light,
The bending of limbs
   that bow in the night.
The power of His being,
   the shout of His stand…
Be still and just listen—
   the world's His command!

Spring!

SPRING in all its splendor
    explodes with passing days,
And brings with it the brightness
    of sun to warm our ways.

Celebrate the season,
    and welcome all that lives...
Greet what is before you—
    enjoy what nature gives!

Embrace each wondrous thing
    that shows a spring-like sign,
And discover all the miracles
    that come forth at this time!

Rain

thirst-time quenching

tree leaves drenching

lifetime giving

wondrous

drops!

Anticipation

Gently blowing breezes
   kiss the early morning day.
Claps of distant thunder
   sound in far off yonder way.

Chirping birds call out their songs,
   while air grows dense and damp.
And rumbles come yet closer still,
   as heaven's drum roll starts.

A first drop there…upon the pane
   Another yet again–
It's coming, yet we know not when.
   Anticipation grows!

     Just then–
     Was that a flash of light?
     Or does imagination run?

Are we prepared and ready
   for the moment once it comes?
Can we, in all our worldly minds,
   embrace what God can give?
Or should we rather just resolve
   to put our trust in Him?

Raindrops

Gentle raindrops
Beating rhythm,

Claps of far off thunder heard.

Eyes closed tightly
Chin tucked covers,

Hush sweet babe—no spoken words.

Window tapping
Puddle making
River filling,

Springtime drops.

Boston Fern

green

firm and regal

each leaf a step

like rungs of a ladder

soldiers standing tall

reaching, stretching

growing!

Promise

Sounds of quiet peace...

Chirping birds call to the day,
    as pairs of turtle doves coo their songs.
Distant whistles of trains
    remind us of places far from heart.
Soft rustling of lush green leaves
    stir sweet smells of fragrance.

A moment to remember,
A feeling to capture...

Warm as a mother's hug,
Soft as the petals of a rose.

It touches the soul with hope and promise!

Time

The softness of a summer breeze
    as floating clouds drift by,
The rustling of the autumn leaves
    while geese fly through the sky.

The sound of rain against the glass,
The pungent smell of fresh cut grass,
The touch of baby's sweet, soft cheek,
The hugs of friends who finally meet.
The heaven's stars on August nights,
October's harvest full-moon light,
The periwinkle sunset sky,
The dawn of golden morning's light.

All this for us to see and feel,
    and know, and have, and do—
A gift from God to us each day,
    with His instructions too!

The joys He sends for us to know
    if we'd just take the time,
To slow our lives and thoughts and deeds...
    such inner peace we'd find!

A Summer's Day

The time, it goes so quickly by,
   the seconds tick away.
The minutes come, the minutes go,
   as we mark off the days.

We tightly cling to that most dear,
   recalling memories past–
And wish for just one moment
   we could make a good time last…

But lives move on and all is changed,
   we never can go back–
Yet just this once, one heartbeat more,
   we'd love to slam that door!

     We'd hold those thoughts
     We'd breathe that air
     We'd pause for one last time…

And try to keep those feelings,
   locked away within our minds.

Dreamin'

Day…and Night…Day…
dreamin' to the quiet sounds of the babbling brook.

A brief moment of memory
A whisper of tomorrow
A touch of hope.

Summer's Eve

The sounds of the evening
    as night gently falls,
Cicadas and crickets and locusts all call.

While gentlest of breeze
    rustles summer's green leaves,
And far away voices give sweet harmony
    to a background of music this summer day's eve.

Treasure these moments
    for they soon shall pass–
Like days from our childhood,
    or clouds floating past.

Our lives must move on
    and the changes will come,
So capture these memories, before they're soon gone!

Red Ribbons

red ribbons of burning flames

stretch across the western sky

screaming, slowly fading,

vibrant horizon

holding on…

sunset!

Twilight

The magic of twilight
   as day softly ends,
The twinkling of fireflies
   and enchantment they lend;

The rustling of tree leaves
   and freshness of a summer breeze,
The croaking sounds within the woods
   and noise of distant voices heard;

Sit still, and take a moment
   to drink the quiet time,
Breathe in the smells of summer
   still fresh upon the mind.

Wish there, upon that distant star,
   your private thoughts of times, afar…
Watch day fade gently into night
   until which time full-moon gives light!

Night Lights

Could there ever be more splendor
    than this August nighttime sky—
The heaven's stars, the crescent moon,
    as darkness shrouds our eyes?

The distant sound of katydids,
    the cricket's lonesome call,
The crisp, cool feel of nighttime air
    that teases us of fall.

Remember when...what once was in
    your hearts and thoughts of old—
Those days long gone, those memories past,
    those feelings you still hold?

Then look again, beyond the dark,
    this starlit August night,
And count those stars, and dream some dreams
    while watching all the lights.

Look high above, look on, look out,
    make *every* star a wish—
Enjoy the moment and the time,
    and cherish this night's gift!

Full September moon,
    hanging high up in the sky—
Shining down so brightly,
    as we dream dreams this night.

The Changing Moon

Dark, yet edged in light...
Promise behind the shadow of questions.

The quiet evening
   reflects the busy day–
Like the warming aftermath
   of burning coals.

A time to reflect...
   while illuminated memories–
        fade
                peacefully
                          away.

Moonlight

October moon, in golden splendor,
    floating in the eastern sky,
Just a sliver of full moonlight
    caught within my lover's eyes.

Brushing tops of tree-lined heavens,
    like a cradle rocking, rocking,
Perfect shape of light before us...
    autumn evening's moonlit night.

Orange harvest moon,
    floating in clouds of sea—
Telling us of futures
    that are yet to be!

October Night

White crescent moon,
   shining in the night,
Just above the tree tops
   hanging low up in the sky.

Cool breezes blowing,
Soft starlight showing,
Bright moonlight glowing,

   Still, October night!

Silver Sliver

The silver sliver of moon
    slides softly away–
Black-ink stillness greets
    the dawning of a day.

Each breath stirs anticipation...
What will come in the new time?

        WATCH...
           LISTEN...

Count the disappearing stars,
    like the moments in our lives.

Passing of Time

Gentle patter of raindrops on golden fallen leaves,
Cool, clean, damp smell of a quiet autumn day,
Soft, rustling leaves mark the passing of time.
Distant chirping of birds call us to the present.

    Ripened walnuts, with spotted outer shells,
        break from their lofty space,
    And pepper the ground where they fall.

    Still, deserted tractors in unfinished fields,
        waiting...

    A moment of peace between seasons.

First Snow

Snow so gently falling, falling,
    melodies of soft white hush,
Whispers from the sky above us
    fill our eyes and chill our touch.

World serenely dressed in silence
    virgin-white to cover all,
Every snowflake charmed with difference
    adds to beauty as it falls!

Winterland

Winter silence, laced with beauty—
stark white color fills my eyes.

Chilling wind and falling snowflakes,
ice-topped trees, and darkened skies.

Just a hint of sun peeks through now—
just a token of what comes.

Soon the storm will pass beyond us,
to reveal the wonders done!

Solace

blanket of white powder frost

fairy-painted wonderland

sparkling winter solace

ice crystal view

crisp serenity

stillness,

broken by one lonely

redbird!

Firelight

The embers burn,
   the hot logs crack,
     as they dissolve to whitened ash.

A transformation on this night
   until, which time, with morning light...

     the air grows chilled,
     and coals are stilled
     with just a hint of memory, 'till–

Once more we stoke and fan the fire,
   to warm our hands
     while flames grow higher.

Awakening

Frosted morn–
  kissed with winter white,
   greets the rising sun.

The hushed calmness
  breaks with forest sounds.

    A day begins.

Come Morning

The calm of winter's beauty
   after last night's storm has passed,
Leaves tree limbs iced with whiteness
   to help the memory last...

While sun shines down so brightly
   reflecting off the snow,
And stirs a warmth within us
   against the nature's cold.

Winter's Chill

Furling smoke pours from the chimneys,
   one lone blackbird in the sky.
Frigid air whips through the treetops,
   bleak white nothing fills our eyes.

Snowmen stand like stiff, straight soldiers—
   stoic souls challenge the chill.
Swirling winds drift snow around us,
   winter's come…against our will!

Peace

Winter solace...
    Trees laden with new fallen snow.

Hushed stillness at the dusk of day.

        Where will we go from here?
        Why do we fret with anticipation?

If only we'd take the time
        to look...
            to see...
                to feel...
                    to absorb...

    The knowledge is here.

The answers are before us
    in the gently falling snow–

        Peace abides,
                LISTEN!

*Blessed is the man who finds wisdom,
the man who gains understanding...
Her ways are pleasant ways,
and all her paths are peace.*

Proverbs 3:13,17

About the Author

Carol Elaine Powell received both her bachelor's and master's degrees in education from Purdue University. As a young child she moved to Indiana, where she still lives today.

Always eager to embrace a new challenge or opportunity, she has been an administrator, author, business owner, carpenter, farmhand, groundskeeper, hair stylist, janitor, manager, model, realtor, sales associate, secretary, step-parent, teacher, wife, and most significant to her, mother.

Her poems, often motivated by personal experiences and influenced by the rural countryside and small town living she enjoys, are an expression of the balance she perceives between God and everyday life.

Her collection of thoughts are both inspiring and thought provoking to the reader.

A Poet's Disclaimer

One day I thought I'd write some verse,
A little book to read...

But dare, I thought, my feelings put
For all my friends to see?

"What if," said I, they were to say
They thought I was no good?

Could then, I be a laughingstock
For all of those who would–

Know of my innermost of soul
And feelings that I hold.

"Oh well," said I, "what if?"..."Here goes!"
"What is the worst to be?"

"A fool," you say, oh my, I guess
The world will have to see!